CHAPTER 1
WHAT IS PUPPY TRAINING

Puppy training will be the method needed to maintain the pup from peeing and generating a mess all more than the floors from the property. It's that basic yet it seriously isn't basic at all. Unlike with the cat and kitten companions learning rapidly to use the litter box, puppy house training requires just a bit much more function. It'll possibly take longer than Wimbledon's longest ever tennis match and maybe even longer than the duration of the World Cup Soccer tournament.

It isn't for your faint of heart. The pup doesn't know instinctively that peeing all around the living room carpet isn't something that may please its new human companions. It has to discover not to accomplish this via both repetitive education and positive reinforcement. And for that record, rubbing the puppy's nose in it seriously isn't a strategy to offer positive reinforcement.

The new pup proprietor has to be patient throughout the puppy house training as it isn't an overnight course of action. The pup learns greatest by means of repetition. The pup requires a drink of water; the proprietor requires the pup outside to try and do his small business. The pup eats dinner; the proprietor will take the pup outside to accomplish his small business.

After the pup does his business outside, the proprietor needs to praise the pup for being such a great pup. The pup will like the praise and will discover that the approach to gain the praise is by doing those actions that have brought the praise prior to. As stated, it is going to not be a quick or overnight practice but the end result in the puppy house training will probably be a pup which has learned to avoid as much as feasible generating a mess inside the household all above the carpet (or all above the clean clothes or wherever else the pup might discover to make the mess.

One other aspect that could support facilitate the puppy training will be the repetition of providing food and water and walks at consistent times throughout the day. While the pup won't, in fact, be capable to read the clock, it is going to study that particular activities in its day occur in a particular order. That's, consume, drink, walk within the morning and consume, drink, walk inside the evening. Or whatever the individual pup parent decides works greatest to the two participants.

The new pup is really a lot of operating but the end result of companionship is worth the effort. Repetition and praise will enable the puppy training to happen and a pup which has received correct puppy house training will likely be a pup capable to maintain its companion happily.

Maltese Puppy Training

You might need to engage in some Maltese puppy training if you've recently acquired one of these fine dogs. This happens to be one of the main places where good bonding with your puppy can occur. He or she will know what you expect of him and you will understand more about how he will react. Underneath we notice some genuinely valid statements about training your Maltese puppy sooner rather than later.

Being originally from Europe, the Maltese breed has been considered to be one of Europe's oldest toy breeds first popular among people with status including aristocracy and other royal subjects.

Starting your Maltese puppy training may be difficult at first at least with respect to house training. After about 21 days, it will probably be helpful to crate train your Maltese puppy. Don't use abrasive techniques when attempting to train your puppy. This remains constant for all dogs, not simply the Maltese breed. In all situations use a calm assertive demeanor in order to show love, gentleness, control, consistency, etc. Use reward in patients as a motivator to get your dog doing what it should.

Maybe before you start out doing formal training for your puppy, a little pretraining will probably be helpful. This exercise will involve getting your puppy to come to you. Make sure your puppy is a fair amount a distance away. At the same time, call your puppy using the "come" command while also clapping and a happy manner. Using a sweet high-pitched voice for this command will help attract your puppy's attention. Once he comes/arrives, reward him with praise and/or a small treat. This exercise can be a really good precursor for future training sessions.

Following basic guidelines in almost any discipline will always be a good idea. This also holds true when attempting to get your puppy to learn. Guidelines, for example, will help you effectively actualize your Maltese puppy training. Follow these guidelines during formal training sessions but also in simple everyday life for your puppy. Your puppy will be constantly learning so if you allow him to learn consistently, he will learn faster.

Consistency will always be very important when it comes to your puppy learning he effectively and quickly. There will be times when you only use audible commands but also other ones where you might use visual cues. In any manner of communication, you need to continually use the same audible or visual signal to ask for a particular action on your puppy's part. For example, if you use the word "come" as a command, only use that word and not others included like "come now".

Using punishment is a big no-no when it comes to training any dog including your Maltese puppy. They simply do not respond very well to punishment. Get your dog to take action by motivating him with praise and rewards. Positive reinforcement really cannot be beaten when it comes to training your puppy.

Remember to challenge your Maltese puppy, first, in simple ways. Later as he matures, you'll want to increase the complexity of a particular challenge. Dogs like a challenge since it brings new experiences in which they can build on. Often, the happier dogs are those that use their brain more.

Thinking about your puppy's attention span will be helpful when seeking to train him effectively. The younger puppy will have a shorter attention span than an older one. At first, you'll want to keep your training experiences short but later as your puppy gets older it will be okay to lengthen those training times.

At any time around your puppy, you want to project a calm assertive demeanor as any proper pack leader would. All dogs including the Maltese are pack animals. They are genetically predisposed to need any leader. That leader has to be you as the master. However, they can include every human in your household. Being the leader requires you've been patient and confident. Please note that if you do not take a position as pack leader, your dog will. When this happens, you will undoubtedly have dog problems.

Think upon timing when training your Maltese puppy. Your puppy needs to know what you mean business when it comes to responding to your commands. In the event that you give the order, your puppy ought to react right away In the beginning, it might take some effort to get your Maltese puppy learning what you want him to learn. This breed generally has been found not to be the easiest one to train. However, like all dogs, the Maltese are very trainable. Training sessions will only strengthen your bond with your puppy. It will make his life and yours much happier.

How To Litter Train You Puppy Easily And Fast

Puppy litter training is the newest trend in puppy training. Litter training is another method for toilet training a puppy. If you live in a high-rise apartment or live in the cold and snowy place you can litter train your puppy. Whatever reason you want to litter train your puppy, it can be done a puppy can be trained to use a litter container just like a cat.

❖ REASONS TO LITTER TRAIN YOUR PUPPY

I have never litter trained my own puppies because I prefer to walk and toilet train my puppy, I understand that certain conditions might prevent puppy owners from walking the puppies regularly enough to get them to toilet train their puppy. If you are elderly and cannot walk long enough or you work long hours and are not able to walk your dog often enough, litter training your puppy can be the best thing for you.

❖ PUPPY LITTER TRAINING BOX CHOICES

Though there are many different puppy litter boxes available from expensive ones, like "Ugodog" or grass turf to toilet train your puppy, to an inexpensive version for your puppy like you would use for a cat. The only difference is that you need to get a bigger box than you would if you have a larger puppy.

❖ THINGS TO CONSIDER WHEN PUPPY LITTER TRAINING

Keep in mind when litter training your puppy that the size of your puppy is going to become a factor. Larger puppies require larger boxes or puppy pads. The reason for this is larger dogs require large boxes, and large dogs end up with... well larger things come out of them. So litter training a large dog might not be the best way to housebreak your puppy. But if you choose to toilet train your puppy with a litter box you need to know how to set up the puppy box.

Setting up your puppy's litter box is much like setting up a litter box for your cats. You need to get a large tray that is big enough for your puppy to maneuver in. Get the same kind of granules that you would buy for your kitty litter box and fill the tray with it. You want to make sure that the tray is deep enough to hold enough granules to enable them to absorb your puppy's urine, yet low enough to allow your puppy to comfortably climb into it and use the toilet. You should get the kind of kitty litter granules that absorb the puppy's urine and form hardened clumps that are easy to scoop out and throw away with the poop.

Teaching your Puppy to Use a Litter can be just as tricky as paper training your puppy. You should use your training crate to hold your puppy until you are sure that he will always go to his litter tray to do his business. This can take a while and as your puppy is outside of the training crate, you need to watch your puppy at first. If you see that your puppy is starting to squat or lift up his leg, you need to direct him to his litter box before he does it. That is the best way.

If you see the mess already, put him in the training crate. Leave him in there for a while. Keep in mind, when your puppy does his business other than in his litter box, tell him "NO!"

Recognition and reward your puppy each time you see him do his business in his litter box. Tell your puppy "great kid" or "great young lady" when he goes to their litter plate without your controlling the person in question. Give him a treat and he will, in the end, discover this is the puppy toilet.

Keeping the litter box clean is critical to make your puppy happy with doing his business in there. The correct granules will harden when they interact with urine. These solid clumps can easily be scooped up and thrown away with a pooper scooper. The proper litter scooper is a sifted scooper, which has slats that allow the dry litter to fall back into the litter tray but hold the clumps that are too big to fall through the slats. This means that you are able to pick up the urine clumps together with the poop and conveniently throw it into the garbage, like with a cat litter box. Ensure that in the wake of cleaning your pooch's litter box, the granules are spread equitably.. You should add new granules occasionally.

Remember. It's all in the litter training. Puppies usually learn quickly if you are persistent. If you choose to litter train a larger dog, you will still need to take him for a walk so that he can get the exercise he needs.

CHAPTER 2
PUPPY TRAINING FOR BETTER BEHAVIOR

Puppy training must be done by every dog owner that wants to have a nice puppy. Sometimes this puppy training can be a difficult process to have if you do not know how to do it. Puppy training needs time and lots of patience from the dog owner. The goal of this puppy training is having an obedient dog.

Having a dog turned out to be prominent since the dog got a predicate as the man's closest companion. Most people choose to have puppies because they are very cute and fun. But do not be misguided by the look, have a puppy the same as having a child. You need to have a great responsibility for all the puppies' needs. Puppy training is one of the most significant occupations for each owner. Here are some of the puppy training.

Dog barking is a common problem when you have a dog. You will have to train the dog to control the barking since they are a puppy. If you just let it barks when he wants it, then it will become a bad habit and difficult to change later. To have barking puppy training, you must create a condition that makes the dog bark with purpose, such as to alarm for intruders or strangers coming in your yard. Never let the puppy to bark without purpose, we need to find the reasons why the puppy is barking. Be patience with this barking puppy training because it needs time and persistence.

You have to teach jumping puppy training for your puppy. Jumping on people is not a good habit to have. When you catch your puppy is going to jump on people, better to stop it immediately, so the puppy will know that it is a forbidden act. Jumping on people can be a serious problem if you have a large dog breed that is strong and heavy enough to knock down a man. Just think when your dog jumps on elder people or small kids, it will be terrible.

Try not to cause the puppy to rely upon you to an extreme. You must train the puppy to be able to stay alone in his kennel or crate. You are not able to stay close with your dog every second, you will need to go work, go shopping, take the kids to school and many other activities that will make your puppy remain alone at the house. So you must make the puppy get used to being alone at home for some time in a day.

A puppy needs to be socialized so it will not afraid to see any strangers when you take him anywhere else outside the house. Socialization puppy training can also support barking training. If your puppy is used to see the mailman or trash truck he will not bark at them when coming. Puppies love to have dog walk, but without better socialization, your dog is going to be afraid to meet so many strangers outside.

So have puppy training as soon as the puppy is ready to have it, do not postpone the training until the puppy gets older when the bad habit is already set it will be more difficult to be changed. Always remember never give physical punishment or yelling at the puppy when your puppy is not following the training instructions. This demonstration will just make your puppy alarm of you

Use These Puppy Training Techniques For Better Success

Puppy training techniques are important assets in raising a puppy. Showing a puppy the aptitudes vital for socialization and submission can help ease the dissatisfactions that accompany having an untrained puppy. Not all doggies are similarly open to training, be that as it may, and finding the strategies that best fit the puppy's needs will guarantee the best result.

Training a puppy requires time and commitment from the owner or mentor. A few young doggies might be normally disposed towards forceful or against social conduct. In such cases, tolerance is vital, and the owner must keep on reinforcing the training regardless of whether the puppy commits rehashed errors. A significant point to consider in dog training is the creature's age. While social issues in completely developed dogs can be remedied with the correct techniques, it is commonly a lot simpler to prepare another puppy or a more youthful dog. On the off chance that conceivable start training the puppy at 6 two months. The puppy's age frequently figures out which training strategies are the most reasonable.

The initial phase in training is to familiarize the dog with its new home and environment. Housetraining includes such puppy training techniques as case training, potty training, and acknowledgment of straightforward directions. The capacity of the puppy to perceive such directions as "sit," "come," and "remain" are particularly significant. These guidelines fill in as a reason for future training and guarantee the wellbeing of the puppy in an open setting.

Socialization is another significant part of puppy training. On the off chance that appropriately mingled, the dog will have the option to connect with different people and creatures without returning to alarmed or forceful conduct. Else, it might be important to sequester the dog to its home consistently to anticipate damage to itself and to other people. The initial three of a dog's life are basic for showing socialization abilities; after the initial 12 weeks, it is essential to reinforce and refine these aptitudes.

Chain training and dutifulness training are basic in instructing a puppy to be polite. Training a puppy to stroll on a chain is twofold: the puppy should initially be fitted with a neckline, and afterward it winds up familiar with a rope. The neckline ought to be a cozy fit yet without being prohibitively so. Chain training enables the owner to walk the puppy securely in an outside setting. Compliance training shows the puppy to react to an order and keeps the puppy from taking part in damaging conduct.

A couple of basic hints can improve the success pace of most puppy training techniques. Training a puppy requires uplifting feedback. Reward the puppy with commendation or infrequent treats when it successfully pursues an order. Encouraging feedback will assist the puppy with bettering ingest the training. Beginning training in an area that is free from interruptions will facilitate the procedure for both the dog and its owner.

CHAPTER 3
THE 6 TIPS ON PUPPY TRAINING

All puppies should be trained, so that they can get along well with their owners, the following tips on puppy training will help you train your puppies.

❖ **TRAIN YOUR PUPPY TO LIE DOWN**

When you train the puppy to lie down in front, you should hold the leash in your left hand. First, let the puppy lie down in front of you, then shake your right hand from the top down, and say "lie down" to him. At the same time, pull the leash down with your left hand to hang his head down and lie the whole body down. If the puppy is unwilling, you can pull his collar down. As well, when you give the command, you can pull his forelegs to be straight before lying down, if he gets it well, give him nice food as a reward at once.

❖ TRAIN YOUR PUPPY TO BRING AND CARRY

There is a training way, in which you can train the puppy easily. Throw a ball and let your puppy bring it back, repeat that again and again. When you throw the ball, say "Bring the ball back" to the puppy. when he gets the ball in his mouth, say "bring" to him. Prepare a little food in your pocket, drop it on the ground when the puppy comes to you. The puppy will open his mouth and drop the ball for the food.

❖ TRAIN TO CALL THE NAME OF YOUR PUPPY

Before training, you must name your puppy firstly. For a good name, you can choose a word one or two-syllable, so that your puppy can remember and distinguish the name. If you have two or more puppies, the pronunciation of the names must be dissimilar, which can avoid confusing your puppies. What's the best time to Call Name Training? in general, it's a suitable time when the puppy's mind is at ease, such as when he is playing or begging for food.

❖ TRAIN YOUR DOG TO HEEL

Our training pays more attention to friendly communication between the puppy and the owner.

1, Get a toy or food which your puppy love with you, let the puppy sit down beside your left leg. Remember that Use the toy or food moves the puppy's attention to you.

2, The owner takes one step forward, tap the left leg, say "Heel" or "Follow" to the puppy.

3, If the puppy is obedient to sit beside you, give him a little food or a stroke as a reward. In addition, keep some space between you and the puppy. when you encourage the puppy, the leash must be loosened, so that puppy knows it's right not to pull the leash.

4, If the puppy runs around, don't worry, call him back and start again.

5, The training time should be limited in 20 minutes. After training, the puppy must be given a lot of fun as a rest, also you can play a game with him.

6, After one week's training, I'm sure the puppy can walk well following you. It's a good beginning, train him frequently, the puppy will follow you adroitly.

❖   PUPPY BARKING

Dog's barking is a natural behavior, the frequency of Dog's barking depends on how you train. Of course, some breeds of dog love barking congenitally, for example, the breed of small, vigorous and alert dog. By comparison, a large dog's dark is deep and powerful, also it's less noisy than a small one's dark.

All puppies should be trained so that they are conscious of when they are supposed to bark and when not. If your puppy dark at the wrong time, you should give him a verbal warning, such as "Hey, be quiet!". If he will be quiet down, give praise to him at once. You're "hey" must be loudly and rigorous.

5 Things You Need For A New Puppy

For a dog lover, there are not many things more energizing than getting another puppy. Regardless of whether you're adopting a puppy from a creature cover or getting a puppy from a reproducer, bringing home another "beloved newborn" is a cheerful day. Be that as it may before you bring home your new puppy you have to prepare. Here are a few supplies you requirement for another puppy to cause his homecoming to go easily.

1. At the top of the list of supplies, you need for a new puppy is your puppy's food. Puppies have a relatively delicate digestive system and it can easily be upset by switching their food suddenly. No matter where you're obtaining your puppy, make sure that you talk to whoever has been feeding him or her and find out what your puppy has been eating. In almost all cases it's best to stick with this diet for the first few days while your puppy is adjusting to your home. There will be enough excitement in your puppy's life during these days without changing his food, too. If your puppy has been growing and doing well on the food he's eating then you will probably want to stay with it. On the other hand, if your puppy has been experiencing any problems with the food - diarrhea, poor coat, not thriving - you will need to change the food slowly. Talk to your vet or experienced dog people about good foods for puppies.

2. Bowls, dishes, pans. Your new puppy will, of course, need some dishware for his meals and a bowl for his water. Stainless steel pans are a good choice. They are easy to clean. They do have the drawback of clanging and moving around easily unless you buy bowls that are weighted on the bottom to prevent them from moving. Ceramic dishes are also a good choice. Make sure that you choose ceramic dishes that are dishwasher-safe if you have a dishwasher. You should steer clear of plastic bowls. Many dogs have a slight allergic reaction to the plastic in the bowls which can lead to bumps and pimples on their muzzles. The plastic in the bowls can also lead to a "snow nose" or make your dog's nose pink instead of dark.

When choosing bowls for your dog it's best to choose a size that's appropriate to your dog's size. If you choose an extremely large bowl for your dog you may be more tempted to overfill it with food which can lead to your dog becoming overweight. If your dog has long ears you may want to get a deep bowl with a small opening at the top so your dog can't get his ears in the food.

Keep your dog's water dish filled at all times and clean it regularly. Dogs don't like dirty water any more than people do. If you have multiple dogs you may want to consider getting a small bucket for their water so you can keep it filled more easily.

3. Collar and leash. Even a young puppy will need a collar and leash. There are many different kinds of collars from which to choose but some of them are intended for training and not for everyday use. Do not allow your puppy to wear a choke chain or slip collar as his normal collar. These are training collars and some dogs - especially young puppies - can get them caught on things and choke themselves. A flat buckle collar is an appropriate collar for a young puppy.

You can also use this kind of collar when you take your puppy to the vet or for walks. Nylon or leather are both fines for this kind of collar but you should remember that you probably don't want to spend a lot of money on a collar for a young puppy since you'll be replacing this collar a couple of times before your puppy is an adult dog. You can get a leash to match the collar. A six-foot leash is a good normal length for walking your dog but you will usually keep your puppy much closer to you and not let him use the full length of the leash.

When fitting your puppy's collar it should fit around his neck and you should be able to slip two fingers between the collar and your puppy's neck. Otherwise, the collar is too tight. A collar that is too loose is also dangerous since your puppy can slip out of it and get loose when you're walking him.

4. Toys and chewies. Each puppy needs toys and safe things to bite on. These are not just luxury things for your puppy! On the off chance that you don't give your puppy toys and chewies, he will completely start to bite on your effects. Give your puppy his own toys and bite things and he will be far more averse to bite on unseemly things like your shoes, furniture, and TV remotes. Give him a decent choice of toys and bites. There are numerous incredible toys for dogs nowadays from basic stuffies to intuitive toys. Bites come in all flavors and in various sorts: rope toys, rawhides, Nylabones, Kongs which can be loaded down with treats, etc. Give your puppy things so he can engage himself and he will be a lot kinder and gentler with your assets.

5. Bed. Your puppy will likewise require a spot to rest. Regardless of whether you enable your puppy to rest alone bed, it's additionally a smart thought for your puppy to have his very own spot. Your puppy needs a spot to go where he can escape from everything. At the point when the house gets boisterous and he needs to withdraw, your puppy needs a tranquil spot to rest. Consider getting a crate for your puppy. Crate training your puppy is constantly a smart thought. It can help with housetraining, with shipping your puppy in your vehicle, and if your puppy ever needs to fly on a plane.

These are the fundamental supplies you requirement for another puppy. You can have these provisions set up before you bring your puppy home. In the event that you plan for your new puppy ahead of time, it will be that a lot simpler for you to enable him to adjust to his new home.

6 Puppy Training Techniques

Knowing some puppy training techniques can be useful to anyone who has a new puppy. If you are finding it difficult to train your puppy, then here are some techniques to use.

First, have some treats. Puppies love to eat tasty treats and they will do anything to get them. You can give your puppy a treat when he did something good, like following your commands. If you continually provide treats, your puppy will surely do the same trick over and over again. On the contrary, if your puppy didn't do anything, you can just ignore him and proceed to train him again.

Second, give verbal praise. This is one of the most essential puppy training techniques that most dog owners should do. Puppies love to be praised for doing a command perfectly. Giving praise is a simple way of saying that you appreciate what your puppy has done. If you do this more often, your puppy will do the same trick, knowing that you will give him appreciation and praise.

Third, start from the basics. Do not teach complicated techniques to your puppy. At first, you have to start from the basics, such as "sit" "stand" and other basic tricks. If you teach complicated tricks first, your puppy will surely get confused.

Fourth, keep the training short and fun. This is another important puppy training techniques to use. Always remember that Puppies do not have the same endurance, like an adult dog. Therefore, you have to keep the training short. Too much training for puppies will easily tire them out, losing focus on every trick you teach them. You should also keep the training fun. Puppies will appreciate learning a trick when playing is involved.

Fifth, patience is one of the most important puppy training techniques.

Keep in mind that training a puppy is like teaching a small child, who doesn't know how to read or write. You should also remember that learning various commands for puppies cannot be achieved overnight. There will be a day where you will find it frustrating to teach your puppy so patience is greatly necessary.

Sixth, know the behavior of your puppy. Look at some of the negative behavior of your dog and see how you can change that. Of course, you can do this by spending quality time with your puppy. The more you spend time, the more you will know about your puppy.

CHAPTER 4

WHAT AGE SHOULD PUPPY TRAINING BEGIN

Numerous individuals are hesitant to begin training their dogs at a youthful age. Regularly individuals imagine that it's smarter to hold up until their puppy is older and maturer before initiating training. Actually sooner you can begin training your puppy the better. A puppy can react to training from as youthful as around 7 weeks old. This article outlines a portion of the issues engaged with training a puppy.

The principal thing to recollect is that dogs are pack animals. Along these lines, your little puppy will quickly begin attempting to work out their position in their pack; ie. your family. In the event that you enable your puppy to run the perch, you're giving out the message that the person is the pack chief. The more you enable your dog to remain in this incredible position, the harder it will be for you to affirm your power once you choose to begin attempting to prepare that person.

A few people feel that beginning to prepare a puppy at a youthful age will remove the enjoyment of having a puppy. This isn't accurate in light of the fact that a significant part of the training procedures utilized for training doggies can be conveyed with regards to the play. While playing you have to hold up until your puppy shows a decent bit of behavior. For instance, you might toss a toy for that person to pursue. On the off chance that the individual gathers this and offers it to you, this ought to be compensated by a treat or heaps of applause. In the long run, you could present the order 'get' to this game.

Keep in mind that little dogs have short fixation ranges, much the same as youngsters. It's important, in this manner, to take training at your puppy's pace. In the event that you start putting a lot of weight on your puppy to react to directions, you may meet an obstruction.

It is additionally important to be extremely persistent with your puppy. In the event that you start getting bad-tempered or forceful while training your puppy, you could wind up with an apprehensive and unusual dog. Attempt to overlook awful behavior (except if your puppy will accomplish something perilous) and center around great behavior. At first, all presentations of good behavior ought to be compensated.

A further urgent component in training a youthful puppy is defining limits. You have to tell your puppy from beginning what behavior is satisfactory and what isn't. It's no utilization giving your puppy a chance to run frantic all around your home, bouncing on everything in locating for a while if this isn't the manner by which you need your dog to carry on in the long haul.

In the event that there is anything you don't need your dog to do, discourage this behavior from the beginning. Along these lines, for instance, on the off chance that you don't need your puppy to get on specific household items, continue lifting the person in question down. In the event that your puppy, at that point approaches the furniture without bouncing upon it - acclaim this behavior.

This article has featured that doggies can begin to react to certain training methods from as youthful as around 7 weeks old. It is recommended that puppy training should begin as ahead of schedule as could be allowed. When training a youthful puppy, the heft of the training ought to be done with regards to the play. Little dogs ought to know about what behavior is worthy and what is unsatisfactory from the earliest starting point. In the event that you start changing the guidelines as your puppy gets older, you'll cause a ton of perplexity. Consequently, the key message is that the prior you begin to advance positive behaviors in your puppy, the simpler it will be to prepare the person in question.

What Your Puppy Needs From You

What does your puppy need to grow up into a sound and healthy dog?

The first thing which comes to mind is good and healthy food.

Proper nutrition is very important for the development of a healthy and strong body. Your pup needs quality food in order to grow.

Your puppy needs its own place.

His bed should be soft and warm and preferably hard to destroy. Or better still, it should not matter whether it gets destroyed or not.

Why not get a cardboard box big enough to make a bed, take one side off and put some soft bedding in? That way you can make sure your pup's bed is of the right size.

When your puppy has reached "full size" you it is still early enough to buy an expensive basket for him.

You know, puppies chew on everything, their teeth are scissor sharp and more often than not a puppy chews and gnaws on something until that something has been shredded.

Getting an expensive bed for your little one is a waste of money and will only frustrate you.

Your puppy needs toys to play with.

Those toys need to be safe. Make sure your puppy can not tear pieces off his toys. Children's toys like teddy bears or such as are not suitable because your puppy can bite plastic pieces like eyes and noses off and swallow them. A puppy's stomach is not the right place for such things. If you get rubber toys the same applies.

Try to avoid squeaky toys as your pup may take the squeaky bit out and swallow it.

If you choose to let your puppy play with your slippers or shoes they will be taken to pieces.

Your puppy needs a collar and lead - using a dog harness is better than using a collar.

Never ever use a choke chain or choke rope for your puppy because of the pain those devices inflict.

But most of all, your puppy needs you!

Your puppy needs your company, your loving voice, the comfort of your body.

Your puppy needs to play with you and to be able to sit and cuddle with you. He needs to sit on your lap, to be part of your life.

Your puppy needs you to be as close as possible so he can bond with you and become your dog.

This is why your puppy does not need a crate, no matter what other people tell you.

If you crate your puppy you frustrate her need to be with you and compromise the bonding process. This will lead to sub-optimal attachment results.

Your puppy needs to create a strong bond with you in order to trust you and to rely on you. Frustrating or hindering his bonding instincts and behavior comes at a price.

Your dog can only make you happy if you keep your puppy happy and fulfill his or her social as well as her emotional needs.

When it comes to rearing a puppy you need to listen to your heart.

Puppies are dogs in the making. A puppy brings joy and happiness into your home but there are a few things you must take care of so your puppy can grow into the dog of your dreams.

Getting to know you well helps your pup to understand you, learning to trust you will help him to follow your commands later in life. Therefore you need to make sure that you always are the just and reliable person your puppy needs you to be. Never let anger or frustration get the better of you when it comes to dealing with your dog, no matter how old he or she is.

CHAPTER 5

TEACHING YOUR PUPPY TO RESPOND TO THE SOUND OF HIS NAME

Does your puppy know his name? Does he respond immediately when you call him? If he doesn't, try training him this easy and fun exercise, and in no time you will have him responding to you immediately each time he hears the sound of his own name.

The usefulness of teaching your puppy to respond positively and immediately to the sound of his name is obvious; for example, training him other basic commands, such as to sit, remain, or rests will be a lot simpler on the off chance that he has his consideration upon you, and not on different things.

Teaching your puppy to respond to his name should be one of the very first lessons he learns, however, in reality, many owners fail to do this effectively early on, and as consequence problems often develop. The analogy I would use would be learning to drive; you need to learn to drive forwards, before learning to drive backward, learning to drive backward, requires a bit more skill, and you need to learn the basics, before you can confidently move on.

By taking advantage of your puppy's natural exuberance, and curiosity, it will make teaching him this exercise a piece of cake!

When you are teaching your puppy this exercise, please try and always remember to teach your puppy to associate this sound with good things only. Don't scold your puppy for example, by using his name, as doing this too often will cause him to build a negative association to the sound, or to become confused, due to the tone you use when saying his name, the latter is more likely to get you the response was your puppy moves away from you, rather than towards you.

To train your puppy this exercise, first gather some things together your puppy enjoys as treats; some puppies are more food motivated, whereas, others prefer toys to play with, work out beforehand what your puppy likes best. My advice would be to attach a long training lead to your puppy at this point, but only if he is first used to wearing a lead and collar, and take him to a quiet area with zero distractions.

Next, lay down on the floor and call his name; call his name in one of that exciting kinds of ways puppies love to hear, and if he looks in your direction give him a food treat or his toy. The objective of this exercise is to eventually have your puppy look directly into your eyes when you call his name, as you will be certain then that you have his complete attention. To help reinforce this behavior, but the food treat or toy up to your face when you call his name, and make eye contact with him when he looks towards the food treat or toy.

The timing here, as with any training you are giving your puppy is important; therefore, try to reward him when you have his attention. This may be difficult at first, as a puppy's movements can be quite erratic, and on occasions, you may reward him at the wrong times, but stick with it and you will improve your timing, and you can put this skill to good use when training your puppy new behaviors.

The next step you need to take is to 'proof' your puppy's behavior. By proofing your puppy's behavior you will test his new skills, and hone them, using different environments, and adding distractions, for example, when the house is busy, or taking him to the local park. A thing to remember here is when you change the environment in which you are reinforcing your puppy's skills, you may encounter some problems initially; for example, he may not be as motivated to look at you when you call his name as much as he was when you trained him this behavior in the house.

Try to remember, he is not being willful, the new environment along with its added distractions will divert your puppy's attention from you, to help counter this, remain patient, and build his concentration gradually again, try not feeding him before you give him session, and using small tasty food treats, such as sausage, meat, or cheese, as a reward for his correct responses.

To recap then, only use your puppy's name along with a positive tone. Never punish, or scold your puppy while using his name. Begin training your puppy this exercise in an environment with no distractions, and build in distractions slowly. Keep your session's short, say for example, no longer than five minutes, and spread them out throughout the day. Give your puppy plenty and plenty of praise for his correct responses, and remember to keep things fun for him, and last of all, always end on a positive note, in this way, your puppy will look forward to his fun and rewarding sessions with you.

Puppy Training Biting

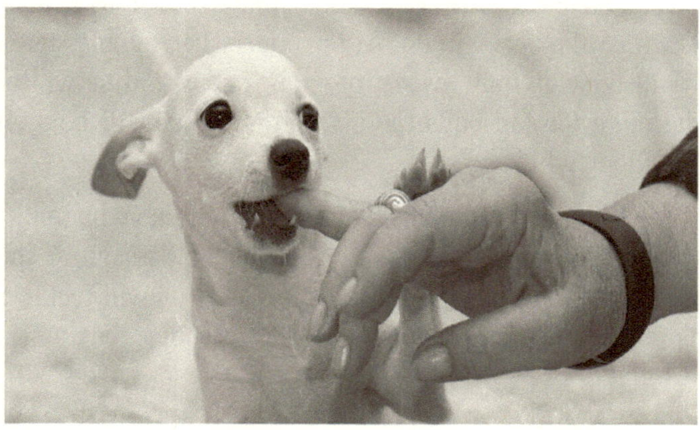

Probably the greatest test that new puppy proprietors face with their puppy training is the puppy training biting stage. It is one of the most stressing pieces of having a puppy particularly on the off chance that you have youngsters. Before we get into the fundamental steps of how to quit biting puppies we have to comprehend your puppy's behavior.

Why Do Puppies Bite?

At the point when puppies are born, they investigate the world through their eyes, ears, feeling of smell and tragically their teeth.

At the point when puppies are in the home for a primary couple of weeks, they will begin to build up their faculties. They will begin to play with the other puppies and will begin playing with the other puppies pursuing, turning over one another and biting one another. They need to be number one in the pack and this is a method for getting to the top, yet in the event that the puppy gets too clamorous, the mum will reprimand them.

So you are presently his mum and you must reprove him.

At the point when your new puppy lands at your home he is presently part of your pack. He needs to get whatever scents and looks great and he will need to give it a decent bite. The issues start when your puppy chooses that your fingers fall into this classification. This is play biting and we have to stop this behavior.

In the event that you have kids, you should plunk down with them and encourage them what they have to do. At the point when puppies bite a kid, the youngster will typically pull away from your puppy and he will believe it's a game, the more the kid pulls the harder the puppy will hold and the better time your puppy will have.

Start until the age of around 4 months, your puppy will have his milk teeth. These teeth are little needles they won't do a lot of damage at this age however as he gets older his teeth will get greater and you will feel it. So we currently comprehend why are puppies bite so we should begin with our Puppy training biting.

HOW ABOUT WE START WITH YOUR PUPPY TRAINING BITING

Perhaps the least complex approach to stop your puppy biting is to roar "ouch" in a profound blunt voice. This will astound him and by and large, he will discharge his hold.

When he gives up offer him a toy, he will discover that he is permitted to bite his toys. Give him a chance to bite the toy for a couple of minutes, at that point take it from him utilizing the order "give".

You should recall not to blow up with your puppy. You may feel worried that your puppy biting is an indication of a poor demeanor. Your puppy's behavior is natural and it will be your business to show your puppy that biting isn't satisfactory in the event that he needs to be a piece of your pack.

Training your new lab puppy to take toys and treats delicately is an incredible method for controlling his behavior. This way your puppy will figure out how carry on in the manner that you need him to. On the off chance that he's great, he will get a treat and commendation.

PUPPY TRAINING BITING THE NEXT STEP

Start off with offering your new puppy a treat. On the off chance that your puppy attempts to snatch it, close your hand and utilize the order "delicately".

Offer the treat once more; if the puppy attempts to snatch it again close your hand once more.

At the point when your puppy demonstrates an improvement compensate him with the treat.

Attempt this few times each day, retaining the treat until your puppy begins to take it pleasantly. Probably the greatest test that new puppy proprietors face with their puppy training is the puppy training biting stage. It is one of the most stressing pieces of having a puppy particularly in the event that you have youngsters. Before we get into the fundamental steps of how to quit biting puppies we have to comprehend your puppy's behavior.

WHY DO PUPPIES BITE?

At the point when puppies are born, they investigate the world through their eyes, ears, feeling of smell and shockingly their teeth.

At the point when puppies are in the home for a principal couple of weeks, they will begin to build up their faculties. They will begin to play with the other puppies and will begin playing with the other puppies pursuing, turning over one another and biting one another. They need to be number one in the pack and this is a method for getting to the top, yet on the off chance that the puppy gets too tumultuous, the mum will reprimand them.

SO YOU ARE CURRENTLY HIS MUM AND YOU MUST CONDEMN HIM

At the point when your new puppy lands at your home, he is currently part of your pack. He needs to get whatever scents and looks great and he will need to give it a decent bite. The issues start when your puppy chooses that your fingers fall into this class. This is play biting and we have to stop this behavior.

On the off chance that you have youngsters, you should plunk down with them and train them what they have to do. At the point when puppies bite a kid, the kid will, for the most part, pull away from your puppy and he will believe it's a game, the more the youngster pulls the harder the puppy will hold and the better time your puppy will have.

start until the age of around 4 months, your puppy will have his milk teeth. These teeth are little needles they won't do a lot of damage at this age however as he gets older his teeth will get greater and you will feel it. So we presently comprehend why are puppies bite so we should begin with our Puppy training biting.

HOW ABOUT WE START WITH YOUR PUPPY TRAINING BITING.

One of the least difficult approaches to stop your puppy biting is to roar "ouch" in a profound rough voice. This will astound him and as a rule, he will discharge his hold.

When he gives up offer him a toy, he will discover that he is permitted to bite his toys. Give him a chance to bite the toy for a couple of minutes, at that point take it from him utilizing the direction "give".

You should recollect not to blow up with your puppy. You may feel worried that your puppy biting is an indication of a poor personality. Your puppy's behavior is intuitive and it will be your business to show your puppy that biting isn't adequate on the off chance that he needs to be a piece of your pack.

Training your new lab puppy to take toys and treats tenderly is an extraordinary method for controlling his behavior. This way your puppy will figure out how to carry on in the manner that you need him to. In the event that he's great, he will get a treat and applause.

❖ PUPPY TRAINING BITING THE NEXT STEP

Startup with offering your new puppy a treatment. On the off chance that your puppy attempts to get it, close your hand and utilize the order "delicately".

Offer the treat once more; if the puppy attempts to get it again close your hand once more.

At the point when your puppy demonstrates an improvement remunerate him with the treat.

Attempt this few times each day, retaining the treat until your puppy begins to take it pleasantly.

Tips To Stop Puppy Biting

Everybody adores little guys, yet when they start biting it might cause problems, so you should stop them from biting when you can. Numerous proprietors don't comprehend that this behavior may prompt problems with dominance and hostility later in the dog's life, regardless of how adorable it may show up when your puppy dog is moving around on the floor.

Actually, nearly all puppies figure out how to stop biting when they are still little. Since they have a great deal of kin in their litter, they rapidly discover that at whatever point they bite, they get chomped back. When a puppy is eight weeks old, it ought to have figured out how to not bite. The issue is generally that the mother does not generally get eight weeks to stop puppy biting.

The Early Days

In the event that you take any puppies home which haven't been with their mother for that initial 8 weeks, or that have not understood that they shouldn't bite, then you should invest energy training puppies not to bite.

First of all. Never hit your dog in response to the bite. On the off chance that they don't believe you're playing, they could wind up frightened of you, creating huge fears and tensions that can cause hostility gives sometime down the road.

To have the option to successfully stop puppy biting, you should comprehend why it's biting. To accomplish this, you have to encourage any great behaviors and discourage any negative behaviors. You ought to be mindful so as to ensure that the puppy realizes you are not messing around. Abstain from wrestling, back-and-forth, or pursue games that may cause nipping by the puppy.

When training puppies not to bite, consistency is fundamental! On the off chance that you urgently need to stop puppy biting, you can't become delicate or given the dog a chance to pull off anything. You're doing this to its benefit.

❖ THE TRAINING

An assortment of classes is accessible for training puppies not to bite that you ought to try out. The coaches will utilize techniques much like what the puppy's mother would've utilized so as to show the puppy that biting isn't middle of the road. It is likewise useful for your puppy to figure out how to associate with other dogs also. It demonstrates your dog to respond well to other dogs in the city and can minimize any hostility they show toward other dogs.

While training puppies not to bite, one of a few significant strategies is to divert the biting to something different, for example, a bone or maybe a bite toy. In the early stages of the training, course any endeavors at biting to something they are permitted to bite for instance a bone. Saying "No!" and giving them another thing to bite and bite will cause them to discover that it isn't all right to bite you, however, that they're permitted to bite the bone or bite toy.

Making a hurt sound if the puppy bites you is likewise an awesome strategy. This would reflect the response a puppy gets when it bites its littermate. The puppy does not have any desire to harm you and by making a little howl or whimper they will realize they have. This ought to be sufficient that the puppy gives up and disregard you. More Pomeranian problems are recorded here.

On the off chance that your puppy is very youthful, training it not to bite is one of the first and most critical exercises it must learn. When the puppy is 10 weeks old, it ought to perceive that biting isn't permitted. It'll make the years to come substantially less upsetting and the danger of potential hostility over the long haul a lot of lower.

CHAPTER 6
FOODS NOT TO GIVE TO YOUR DOG

While it is enticing to impart your food to your fuzzy relative, you ought to know that a large number of human foods are poisonous for dogs. You ought to abstain from requesting foods for your dog from the underneath menu.

❖ **APPETIZERS**

Baby Food - Many individuals attempt to give baby foods particularly to little guys when they are not feeling great. Baby foods are not awful when all is said in done. Be that as it may, you should ensure the baby food you are giving doesn't contain any onion powder. Likewise, baby foods don't contain all the important supplements for a healthy dog.

Chewing Gum - Most chewing gum contains a sugar called Xylitol which has no consequences for humans. Notwithstanding, it can cause a flood of insulin in dogs that drop a dog's glucose to a risky level. On the off chance that your dog eats an enormous number of gums, it can damage the liver, kidney or more terrible.

Candy - Many of the candies additionally contain Xylitol, a similar sort of sugar as Chewing gum. In this way, ward off candies and chewing gums from the compass of your dogs and little dogs.

Chocolate - Chocolates are considered poisonous for dogs. Chocolates contain caffeine and theobromine which can be dangerous for your dog. Chocolates can cause gasping, vomiting, and looseness of the bowels, and damage your dog's heart and sensory systems.

Corn On The Cob - Dogs can eat Corn, yet not the cob. Most dogs can't process cob effectively, which can cause intestinal deterrent, an intense and perhaps fatal medical condition if not treated right away.

Macadamia Nuts - Macadamia nuts otherwise called Australia Nuts can cause weakness, sorrow, vomiting, tremors, and hyperthermia in dogs.

Mushrooms - Mushrooms are dubious. While a few kinds of Mushrooms are fine, others can be dangerous to dogs. A few sorts of mushrooms can cause genuine stomach issues for dogs. As a mindful dog owner, you should attempt to abstain from offering mushrooms to your dog.

Tobacco - Never offer tobacco to your dog. The impacts of nicotine on dogs are considerably more regrettable than humans. The lethal degree of nicotine in dogs is 5 milligrams of nicotine for each pound of body weight. In dogs, 10 mg/kg is conceivably deadly.

Cooking Dough - Raw bread dough made with live yeast can be risky whenever ingested by dogs. At the point when the raw dough is gulped, the warm, damp condition of the stomach gives a perfect domain to the yeast to increase, resulting in an expanding mass of dough in the stomach. The development of the stomach might be serious enough to diminish the bloodstream to the stomach divider, resulting in the demise of tissue.

Rotten Food - Spoiled food have shape and other bacteria that can make genuine damage to your dog's health.

- ❖ **MAIN ENTRIES**

Cooked Bones - While raw bones are gainful for your dog's teeth, cooked bones can be hazardous for your puppy. Cooked bones are increasingly fragile, which means it is almost certain they may chip and make interior damage your dog.

Cat Food - A little cat food eaten by your dog may not be an issue. In any case, you feed cat food routinely to your dog, it can cause some health issues. Cat foods typically have a more significant level of protein and fat which are not healthy for dogs.

Fat Trimmings - Meat fat trimmings, cooked or raw can cause pancreatitis in dogs.

Liver - Feeding liver incidentally may be OK, yet don't bolster an excessive amount of liver to your dog. Inordinate utilization of the liver can unfavorably influence your dog's muscles and bones.

Yeast - As referenced prior, a lot of yeast could burst your dog's stomach and digestive organs.

Dairy Products - Some dogs would approve of dairy products. Nonetheless, dogs by and large have moderately poor levels of resilience to lactose which is found in milk. Thus, it can cause looseness of the bowels and other stomach related problems.

- ❖ **DRINKS**

Alcohol - You ought not to let your dog taste any sort of alcohol, not to mention devour it in a huge amount. The main fixings utilized in beer, wine, and other alcoholic refreshments are toxics and hazardous for dogs. Alcohol can cause poor breathing, anomalous acridity, intoxication, absence of coordination and even trance-like state and/or demise for a dog.

Coffee - Too much Coffee can be poisonous for your dog. Regular indications of a coffee overdose incorporate vomiting, tremors, eagerness and fast pulse. In extreme cases, seizures can show up. It's workable for dogs to fall if high amounts of caffeine have been expended.

Milk - Many dogs particularly young doggie drink milk. Most dogs may not experience any issues with milk, yet a few dogs might be prejudiced to lactose found in milk. Dogs sensitive to lactose may experience upset belly and other hypersensitive responses subsequent to drinking milk.

Citrus Oil Extracts - Oil extricates from citrus fruits, for example, oranges, lemons, and limes can cause aggravation in your dog's stomach related framework particularly whenever expended in enormous amounts. Dogs may experience the runs, vomiting, slobbering, and trembling.

❖ **FRUITS AND SALADS**

Apple Seeds - Apple seeds contain amygdalin, a type of cyanide. It can prevent blood from conveying oxygen all through the body. Fend off your little guy from apple seeds.

Avocado - Avocado natural product, its pit, and plant are poisonous for dogs. Avocado damages heart, lung and other tissue in dogs notwithstanding stomach upset, vomiting and pancreatitis.

Grapes and Raisins - Dogs normally get hypersensitive responses in the wake of eating grapes and raising. Dogs may experience vomiting, fatigue, loose bowels, and perhaps kidney disappointment.

Onions - Onions are perilous for dogs. Attempt to abstain from feeding onions (raw or cooked) to your dog. In the event that the dog eats a limited quantity of onions consistently for a long time, it might bite by bit create pallor over weeks to months.

Chives - Chives can cause hemolysis, sickliness, or hemoglobinuria in your dog. A portion of the indications of an excess of chives utilization incorporates weakness, torpidity, pale mucous films, and stained (red to dark-colored) pee.

Peaches - Dogs may not experience any issues in the event that they simply expend peach substance. In any case, pits of peaches are poisonous to dogs. They may make your dog experience expanded understudies, dizziness and unnecessary slobbering.

Plums - Stems, leaves, and seeds of plums are poisonous for dogs. Dogs may experience block red mucous layers, enlarged students, trouble breathing, gasping, and stunning.

Tomato Leaves - The leaves of a tomato plant contain glycoalkaloids alpha-tomatine and dehydrotomatine which are poisonous for dogs. A portion of the side effects of eating tomato leaves incorporate; slobbering, stomach upset, loose bowels, vomiting and changes in his conduct. Tremors or seizures could likewise happen if your puppy has devoured an excessive amount of tomato leaves.

❖ FISH

Raw Fish/Fish as a rule - Some measure of fish in your dog's eating regimen may not create any issues. In any case, If fish are encouraged only or in high amounts to your dog can bring about thiamine (a B nutrient) insufficiency prompting the loss of hunger, seizures, and in extreme cases, passing.

❖ SIDE DISH

Human Vitamins - Some human vitamins can be dangerous for pets, specifically, those that are fat dissolvable like vitamins A, D and E. Additionally, iron tablets can damage the stomach related framework lining, and demonstrate poisonous for the liver and kidneys of your dog. Along these lines, fend off your vitamins from your dog particularly little dogs.

Human Snacks - Some of the human snacks may utilize fixings, for example, onion and garlic powder, raisins, chocolate which could be dangerous for dogs. Attempt to give your fuzzy companion snacks and treats made only for them as opposed to sharing yours.

On the off chance that your dog has a crisis in the wake of eating or drinking something if you don't mind call your veterinarian right away.

www.ingramcontent.com/pod-product-compliance
Lightning Source LLC
Chambersburg PA
CBHW021404160726
47994CB00007B/3065